SIMPLE MACHINES

THE WAY THEY WORK

PHYSICS BOOKS FOR KIDS

Children's Physics Books

BABY PROFESSOR
EDUCATION KIDS

Speedy Publishing LLC
40 E. Main St. #1156
Newark, DE 19711
www.speedypublishing.com

n this book, we're going to talk about the way simple machines work. So, let's get right to it!

Old style pulley.

WHAT IS A SIMPLE MACHINE?

The Greek philosopher Archimedes was the first to describe how simple machines work in 260 BC. Simple machines don't have motors. A simple machine helps you perform work and accomplish a specific task by increasing the strength of a force or by changing a force's direction. Motorized machines are typically made up of numerous simple machines. For example, a car has wheels and axles. It also has pulleys in its engine.

WHAT ARE THE SIX DIFFERENT TYPES OF SIMPLE MACHINES?

During the period of the Renaissance in Italy, scientists defined six different types of simple machines. They are:

- **THE LEVER** - A playground seesaw is an example of a lever.

- **THE WHEEL WITH ITS AXLE** - The wheels on a toy wagon are examples of wheels with axles.

PULLEY

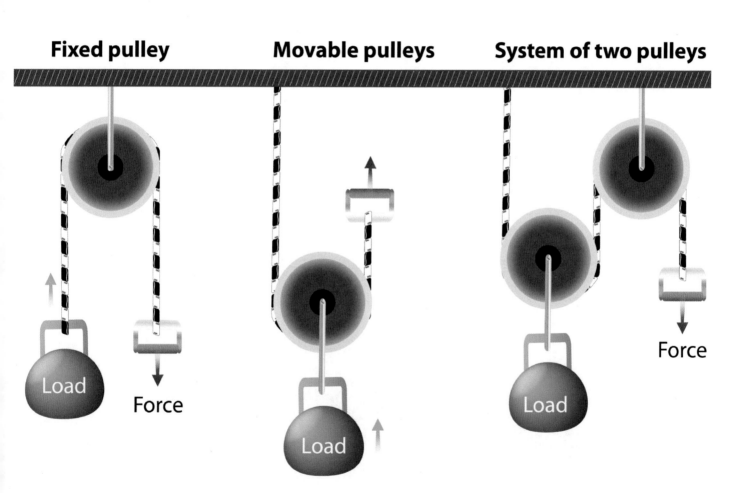

Fixed pulley

Load

Force

Movable pulleys

Load

System of two pulleys

Load

Force

INCLINED PLANE

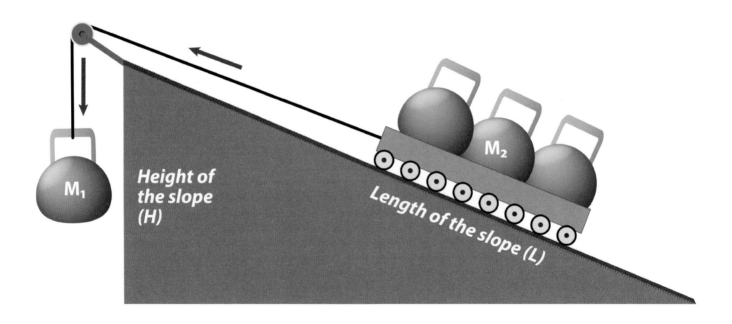

- **THE PULLEY** - A flagpole uses a pulley to lift a flag into position.

- **THE INCLINED PLANE** - Movers use ramps, one type of inclined plane, to move furniture and heavy boxes.

- **THE WEDGE** - Formed by two inclined planes that meet and form a sharp edge, wedges are used to drive things apart or put them back together.

- **THE SCREW** - A jar lid that you unscrew to open a jar is an example of a type of screw.

Screw with cogwheel.

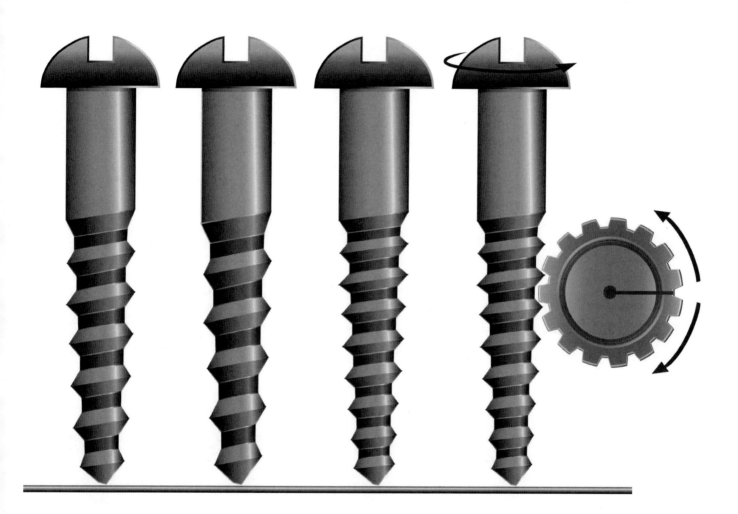

Mother and son going down the slide, a form of inclined plane.

WHAT IS MECHANICAL ADVANTAGE?

You can think of a simple machine as having input force, and then some resulting output force. The ratio of the amount of the input force compared to the amount of the output force is called the *mechanical advantage.* When using a simple machine, you still have to exert some force. You can't get any results if you don't input some force since the machine doesn't have its own motor. However, having the simple machine to help you definitely gives you the advantage. It helps you to accomplish the work faster and with less strain, because it multiplies your input force.

Let's look at an example.

Example:

A construction worker uses a straight, flat board and a log to lift a very heavy rock. This is an example of a simple lever. The input or effort arm, the distance measured on the board from where he is pushing down to where the log is located, is 4 meters.

Levering a boulder.

The output arm or load arm, the distance along the board from the fulcrum, which is the log, to the heavy rock is 1.6 meters. What is the mechanical advantage of the lever the construction worker has created?

Solution:

$$\text{Mechanical advantage} = \frac{4 \text{ meters}}{1.6 \text{ meters}} = 2.5$$

Lever, vintage engraved illustration.

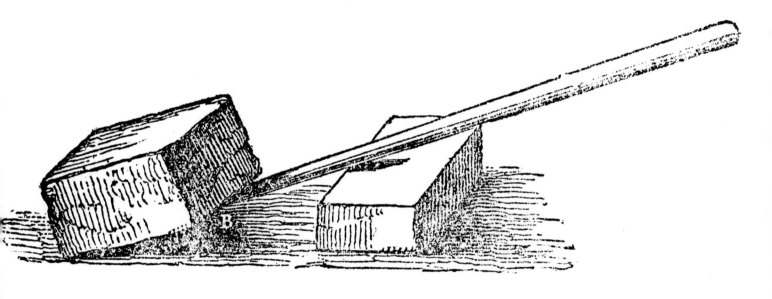

The Simple Lever

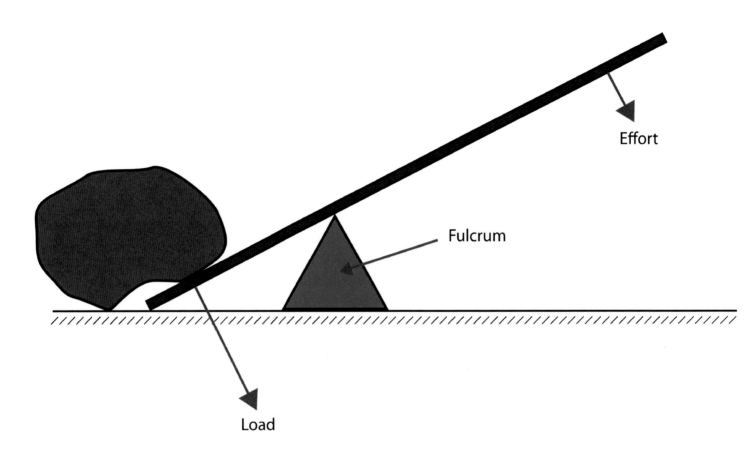

Mechanical Advantage	Velocity Ratio	Efficiency
Mechanical Advantage = $\frac{Load}{Effort}$ (M.A.)	Velocity Ratio = $\frac{\text{distance moved by the effort}}{\text{distance moved by the load}}$ (V.R.)	% Efficiency = $\frac{\text{Mechanical Advantage}}{\text{Velocity Ratio}}$ X 100%
The mechanical advantage describes how much the force is magnified. The M.A. depends on friction.	The effort distance is always further than the load distance. The velocity ratio does not depend on friction.	The efficiency is always less than 100% because of friction. Energy is lost as heat.

This means that, by using the lever, the construction worker was able to multiply his input force by 2.5 times. The result was that it was a lot easier to move the rock than if he had picked it up himself.

Question: What would happen if the input arm were longer? Would it make it easier to move the rock or not?

Solution: It would make the rock easier to move because the force would be greater. For example, if the input arm were 8 meters long, the mechanical advantage would be 5 times the input force.

This is what the Greek philosopher Archimedes meant when he said if he was given a lever long enough and a fulcrum where he could place it, then, he would be able to move the world.

A group of men leverages to overturn a monument of a king on horseback.

Happy little three years old child riding seesaw with big smile.

THE LEVER

There are examples of levers all around. A playground seesaw is an example of a lever. So are pairs of pliers or tweezers or crowbars. A pair of common kitchen scissors is a type of lever as well. As you saw in the example of the construction worker, you can make your own lever from a flat board and a log.

Since people generally apply force to levers, the words "effort" and "load" are sometimes used in place of input force or output force. An input force, also called effort, is applied by the person. That force results, in either the lever moving the load or applying the resulting output force to the load.

There are three different types of levers.

Type 1 Lever

In a Type 1 lever, the effort required the move the load and the load itself are separated by the fulcrum. In other words, you're pushing on one side, there is a fulcrum or pivot in the center, and the load is on the other side. A seesaw is an example of this type of lever.

Men levering a boulder.

So is the makeshift board and log that the construction worker used in the previous example. It's not as easy to see this, but scissors and pliers are examples of two type 1 levers used together. If you look more closely at a pair of scissors you'll easily see the pivot where the two type 1 levers move.

Type 2 Lever

In a Type 2 lever, the load is in a different position than it was in the Type 1 lever.

This time the load is between the effort and the pivot or fulcrum. This one is easy to understand if you think about the way a wheelbarrow works. You lift the handles up, the load is inside the wheelbarrow, and the wheels, which are the fulcrum, are positioned after the load. Not as easy to understand are staplers and bottle openers.

Yellow wheelbarrow.

These are type 2 levers as well. A nutcracker uses two type 2 levers together and so do nail clippers.

Walnut and nutcracker.

Type 3 Lever

In a Type 3 lever, you apply the effort in between the pivot or fulcrum and the load. Staplers, brooms, and tweezers are examples of type 3 levers. Tweezers use two type 3 levers.

Black office hole punch with paper.

Line of old wooden wagons.

THE WHEEL AND AXLE

The wheel is one of the most important inventions the world has ever known. Prior to the invention of this simple machine, human beings couldn't transport much very quickly over land. Imagine how difficult it would be if you had to carry things wherever you had to take them or had to walk to wherever you wanted to go.

WHEEL and AXLE
(simple machines)

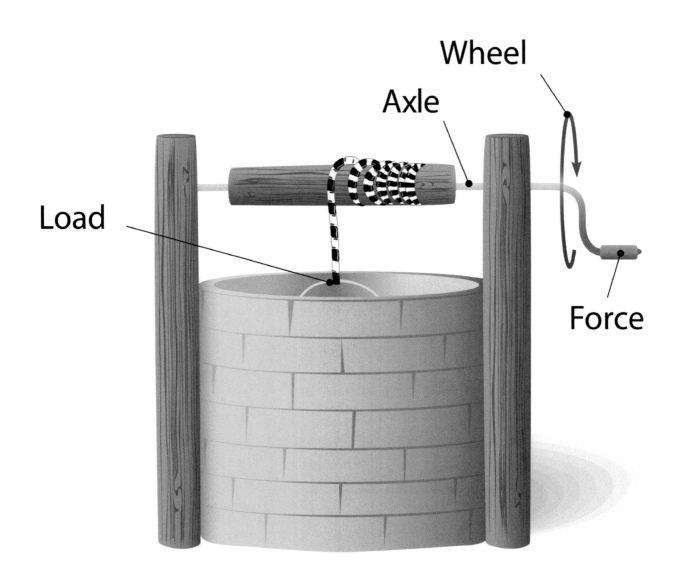

Wheel

Axle

Load

Force

A wheel is actually a special type of lever. Its center acts as the fulcrum or pivot.

Wheels work by decreasing the friction that an object encounters when it's moved across a surface. Think about a file cabinet that's filled with paper. It would take a lot of effort to move that cabinet across the floor, but with four wheels underneath it, it won't be that difficult at all.

Wheels became even more valuable after the Sumerians figured out how to attach an axle to a wheel around 3200 BC. This innovation led to the creation of carts and wagons for transportation of goods and chariots for warfare. Eventually, it led to the creation of the modern-day car, which has a motor as well as wheels and axles. A toy wagon and a Ferris wheel are two examples of wheels and axles.

Stone wheel object as an early invention of the prehistoric era.

A pulley has a wheel that's constructed with a groove in it. A rope fits into that groove. You pull on one end of the rope and then the pulley helps you lift the load, which has been tied with the other end of the rope. The way a pulley works is by assisting you to change the position of the load or change the direction of the force you're applying.

Wooden cart.

Flagpoles as well as window blinds use pulleys. Multiple pulleys can also be used together. A flat wheel used with belts is another type of pulley that's used inside the motors of cars.

With a pulley, you can create more lifting power by wrapping the rope around the wheels more than once. If the pulley has four wheels, the pulley works as if you had four ropes holding the load. You can lift four times the amount, but the catch is, you have to pull on the rope four times as far!

A close up of two wooden handles on window blinds.

INCLINED PLANE
(simple machines)

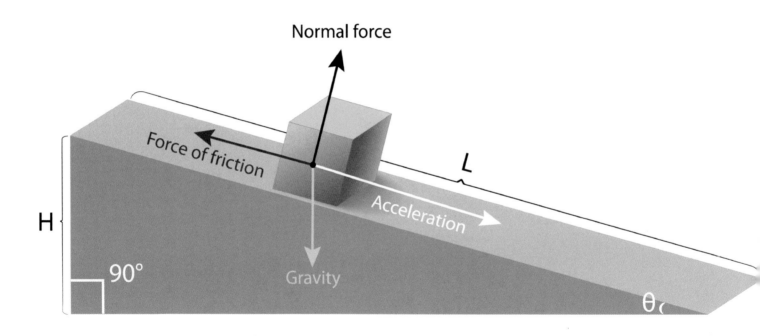

Normal force

Force of friction

Acceleration

L

H

90°

Gravity

θ

$$\text{Mechanical advantage (MA)} = \frac{\text{Length of the slope (L)}}{\text{Height of the slope (H)}}$$

THE INCLINED PLANE

An inclined plane, often called a ramp, makes it easier to move heavy loads. One of the best examples is the ramp that movers use to get things inside their trucks. Instead of lifting everything a considerable height off the ground, ramps can be used to lighten the load. They provide a way for the load to be moved at an angle to the ground. Another example of an inclined plane is a playground slide.

THE WEDGE

If you position two inclined planes with their backs against each other, the result is a wedge. Inclined planes are stationary, but wedges move to do their work. For example, a stonemason might use a chisel to break two pieces of stone apart. An axe used to chop wood is another example of a wedge. Another wedge that you might have in your house is a doorstop. It's a wedge that prevents a door from moving.

WEDGE
(one of the six simple machines)

Force

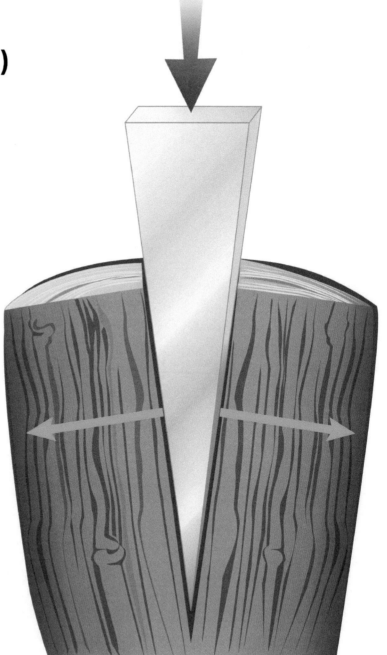

A downward force produces forces perpendicular to its inclined surfaces

SCREW
(simple machine)

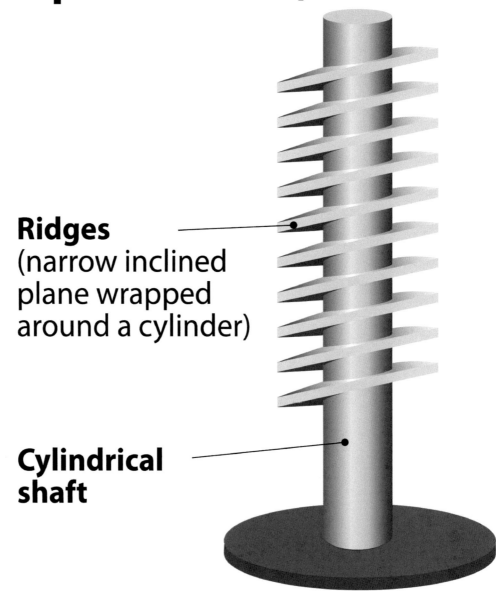

Ridges
(narrow inclined plane wrapped around a cylinder)

Cylindrical shaft

THE SCREW

When you turn a screw, it drills down into wood. If you look carefully at how a screw is designed, you'll see that it's actually an inclined plane that's wrapped around a center pole.

Examples of screws are the type of wood screw you use with a screwdriver, the lid of a jar that screws on and off, and a wine bottle opener.

Awesome! Now you know more about simple machines. You can find more Physics books from Baby Professor by searching the website of your favorite book retailer.

Visit

BABY PROFESSOR
EDUCATION KIDS

www.BabyProfessorBooks.com

to download Free Baby Professor eBooks
and view our catalog of new and exciting
Children's Books

Made in the USA
Coppell, TX
01 September 2020